P9-DCV-093

Welcome to the Reading/Writing Workshop

Explore new ideas!

Read and reread exciting literature or informational texts!

Become an expert writer!

Use what you have learned to unlock the Wonders of reading!

(tl)Ariel Skelley/Blend Images/Corbis; (rt) Tanya Constantine/Blend Images/Getty Images; (b) Kenneth Spengler; (b) Nathan Love

Go Digital! www.connected.mcgraw-hill.com
Explore your Interactive Reading/Writing Workshop.

 Mc Graw Hill Education

Bothell, WA • Chicago, IL • Columbus, OH • New York, NY

Cover and Title Pages: Nathan Love

www.mheonline.com/readingwonders

C

The *McGraw·Hill* Companies

 Education

Copyright © 2014 The McGraw-Hill Companies, Inc.

All rights reserved. No part of this publication may be
reproduced or distributed in any form or by any means, or
stored in a database or retrieval system, without the prior
written consent of The McGraw-Hill Companies, Inc., including,
but not limited to, network storage or transmission, or
broadcast for distance learning.

Send all inquiries to:
McGraw-Hill Education
Two Penn Plaza
New York, New York 10121

ISBN: 978-0-02-119729-3
MHID: 0-02-119729-6

Printed in the United States of America.

8 9 DOW 17 16 15 14

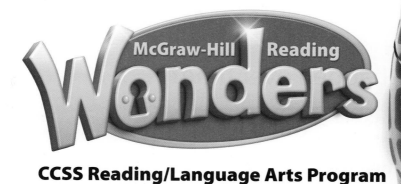

McGraw-Hill Reading
Wonders

CCSS Reading/Language Arts Program

Program Authors

Diane August

Donald R. Bear

Janice A. Dole

Jana Echevarria

Douglas Fisher

David Francis

Vicki Gibson

Jan Hasbrouck

Margaret Kilgo

Jay McTighe

Scott G. Paris

Timothy Shanahan

Josefina V. Tinajero

 **Education**

Bothell, WA • Chicago, IL • Columbus, OH • New York, NY

Unit 3

Changes Over Time

The Big Idea
What can happen over time? **6**

(t) Cathy Delanssay; (c) Kenneth Spengler; (b) Dan Andreasen

4

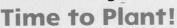

(t) Anna Vojtech; (c) North Wind/North Wind Picture Archives; (b) Tanya Constantine/Blend Images/Getty Images

The Big Idea

What can happen over time?

Changes Over Time

Changes, Changes

Little by little, day by day,
Things grow and change in
every way.

Trees get taller and touch the sky,
Eggs hatch new birds who
learn to fly.

A puppy born in spring is small,
But he'll be bigger when it's fall.

I'm also growing, bit by bit,
Just see—my clothes no
longer fit!

—by George Samos

Cathy Delanssay

Essential Question

How do we measure time?

Go Digital!

COLLABORATE

Talk About It

What are these children learning to do?

Ariel Skelley/Blend Images/Corbis

All About Time

away

Do all birds fly **away** in fall?

now

It's time for us to eat **now**.

some

Some kids like to wear a watch.

today

It is my birthday **today**!

way

A clock is one **way** to tell time.

why

Why is summer a fun season?

COLLABORATE

Your Turn

Say the sentence for each word. Then make up another sentence.

Go Digital! Use the online visual glossary

(tl) Sean Duan/Flickr/Getty Images; (cl) BlueMoon Stock/Alamy; (bl) Shiyana Thenabadu/Alamy; (tr) UpperCut Images/Alamy; (cr) Comstock Images; (br) Fuse/Getty Images

Long a

The a_e spelling makes the long a
sound in **wake**.

date   whale   shakes

wave   safe   plate

snake   game   grapes

trades   vase   brave

Kenneth Spengler

Read Together

Dave gave Jane a plate of grapes.

Can the ants take the grapes?

COLLABORATE

Your Turn

Look for these words with long a spelled a_e in "Nate the Snake Is Late."

Nate	snake	late	make
wade	lake	wake	gaze
lane	gate	Tate	

Essential Question

How do we measure time?

Read about how Nate the snake keeps track of time.

Go Digital!

Kenneth Spengler

14

Nate the Snake Is Late

It is 8 o'clock, and I can not be late.

I do not wish to make my pals wait.

Kenneth Spengler

I must be there at half past ten.

But I have lots of time until then.

Kenneth Spengler

At last I am set and on my **way** there,

But I think I still have **some** time to spare.

I wade in this lake as frogs
hop **away**.

I do not think they wish to play!

The sun is hot, and I nap on a rock.

Then I wake up and gaze at the clock.

Kenneth Spengler

Drats! It is 10 o'clock. Can it be?

Will my pals still be there for me?

I dash up a lane and past the gate.

I am on my way, but am I late?

Kenneth Spengler

My six best pals sit with Miss Tate.

I tell them all **why** I am late.

They grin at me and then they say,
"**Now** we can hear the story **today**!"

Character, Setting, Plot

A **character** is a person or an animal in a story. The **setting** is where and when a story takes place.

The **plot** of a story is what happens at the beginning, middle, and end.

 Find Text Evidence

Find out what happens at the beginning of the story.

page 16

It is 8 o'clock, and I can not be late.

I do not wish to make my pals wait.

Kenneth Spengler

24

Beginning

Nate wakes up at 8 o'clock. He does not want to be late.

Middle

Nate does many things, such as wade in the lake. Then he takes a nap.

End

Nate gets to the library late for story hour. But his friends wait for him.

Your Turn

Talk about the plot of "Nate the Snake Is Late."

Go Digital! Use the interactive graphic organizer

25

 # Readers to...

Word Choice

Kate wrote a poem. She used sensory details to tell how she looks, feels, and sounds when she's late.

Kate's Poem

When I am late,

I race, zoom, and dash.

I huff and I puff

As quick as a flash!

COLLABORATE

Your Turn

Tell what sensory details Kate used in her poem.

Writers

Verbs The words **race**, **zoom**, and **dash** are **verbs**, or action words. You can use commas to separate three verbs.

I race, zoom, and dash.

Your Turn

COLLABORATE

- What verbs did Kate use?
- Write a poem. Use commas to separate three verbs.

Kenneth Spengler

(bkgd) Masterfile; (inset) Jonathan Kitchen/Photographer's Choice RF/Getty Images

Weekly Concept Watch It Grow!

Essential Question

How do plants change as they grow?

 Go Digital!

 **Talk About It**

What does the boy see growing? How will it change?

Ready, Set, Grow!

green

Peas and beans are **green**.

grow

Plants get big when they **grow**.

pretty

The flowers are **pretty** colors.

should

Which seeds **should** I plant?

together

Together we can pull the weeds.

water

Water comes out of the hose.

COLLABORATE

Your Turn

Say the sentence for each word. Then make up another sentence.

Go Digital! Use the online visual glossary

(tl) Goodshoot/Alamy; (cl) Image Source/Alamy;
(bl) FogStock/Alamy; (tr) Pixtal/age fotostock;
(cr) Ariel Skelley/Blend Images/Getty Images;
(br) Huntstock/the Agency Collection/Getty Images

Long i

The i_e spelling makes the long i sound, as in **bite**.

likes	**white**	**five**
whines	**wide**	**size**
ripe	**hide**	**time**
drives	**prize**	**shine**

Dan Andreasen

Five fine pumpkins are on a vine.

What size is the prize pumpkin?

Your Turn

COLLABORATE

Look for these words with long i spelled i_e in "Time to Plant!"

time	Mike	White	fine	five
shines	vines	like	while	
bite	ripe	piles	yikes	

Essential Question

How do plants change as they grow?

Read about how vegetable plants grow.

Go Digital!

Dan Andreasen

34

Time to Plant!

Cast

Beth

Mike

Gramps

Dad

Mom

Miss White

Narrator

Dan Andreasen

Beth: Dad, can we plant a garden?

Dad: Yes! That will be fine!

Gramps: We can plant vegetables.

Mike: Yum! Let's do it **together**.

Dan Andreasen

Mom:	Dad and I will dig.
Mike:	I will drop in five seeds.
Gramps:	I will set in **green** plants.
Beth:	And I will get **water**!

Narrator: Days pass. The sun shines.
Rain plinks and plunks.

Beth: I can spot buds on the vines!

Dad: Sun and water made
them **grow**.

Narrator: Days pass. The sun shines. Rain drips and drops.

Beth: The vegetables got big!

Dad: We **should** pick them.

Mom: Yes, it's time!

Dan Andreasen

Mike: I like to munch while I pick.
I will take a bite. Yum!

Gramps: Sun and water made
them ripe.

Narrator: They pick piles and piles.

Beth: Yikes! That's a lot!

Mike: We can't eat them all.

Gramps: I think I have a plan.

Dan Andreasen

Mike: This bag is for you.

Miss White: They are such **pretty** vegetables! Thank you!

Beth: Sun and water made them grow.

Sequence

Events in a story or a play happen in a certain order, or **sequence**. The events are the plot of the story.

 Find Text Evidence

Find the first thing that happens in "Time to Plant!"

page 37

Beth:	Dad, can we plant a garden?
Dad:	Yes! That will be fine!
Gramps:	We can plant vegetables.
Mike:	Yum! Let's do it **together**.

Dan Andreasen

44

First

The family plants a garden.

Next

The plants get big and grow.

Then

The family picks the vegetables.

Last

They share their vegetables.

Your Turn

COLLABORATE

Talk about the plot of "Time to Plant!"

Go Digital! Use the interactive graphic organizer

Readers to...

Word Choice Ike wrote what he thinks about a play. He picked just the right words to tell about it.

Ike's Opinion

The play tells a happy story.

Kids tend a garden.

Kids share yummy vegetables.

It makes me smile!

COLLABORATE

Your Turn

Tell which of Ike's words were good choices for his opinion.

Writers

Present-Tense Verbs When a verb tells about one person or thing, it ends in **-s** or **-es**. When a verb tells about more than one, it does not end in **-s** or **-es**.

The play **tells** a happy story.

Kids **tend** a garden.

Your Turn

COLLABORATE

- Find another sentence in Ike's writing that tells about more than one.
- Write what you think about a play, book, or movie. Use sentences that have verbs that end in **-s** or **-es**.

Dan Andreasen

47

Essential Question

What is a folktale?

Go Digital!

Adam Taylor/Digital Vision/Getty Images

Story Time

Talk About It

What are these children acting out?

any

Do you have **any** fairy tales?

from

Gram read to us **from** her book.

happy

I am **happy** to be in the play.

once

Once upon a time there was a queen.

so

That story is **so** funny!

upon

Once **upon** a time there was a king.

Your Turn

COLLABORATE

Say the sentence for each word. Then make up another sentence.

Go Digital! Use the online visual glossary

(tl) Shalom Ormsby/Blend Images/Getty Images; (cl) Jakob Helbig/Digital Vision/Getty Images; (bl) Dirk Anschutz/Stone/Getty Images; (tr) Matthieu Spohn/PhotoAlto Agency RF Collections/Getty Images; (cr) REB Images/Blend Images/Getty Images; (br) Brand New Images/Stone/Getty Images

Soft c and Soft g

The letter c can make the soft c sound you hear in **race**.

The letters g and dge can make the soft g sound you hear in **age** and **edge**.

face	place	space
nice	slices	cents
page	cage	stage
pledge	fudge	gem

Anna Vojtech

Madge eats a big slice of fudge.

Gen likes to sing on a stage.

Your Turn

Look for these words with soft c and soft g in "The Nice Mitten."

nice	Lance	edge
mice	place	raced
hedgehog	space	trace

Essential Question

What is a folktale?

Read the story of a little boy's lost mitten.

Go Digital!

Anna Vojtech

The Nice Mitten

Anna Vojtech

Once upon a time, a boy named Lance went out to pick up sticks. His mom gave him nice red mittens in case his hands got cold.

56

"Take the mittens and keep them safe," his mom said. But as Lance left, he ran fast and lost a mitten at the edge of the wide forest.

Five mice saw the mitten. "This is a nice place to rest," they said. **So** the **happy** mice went in and rested.

Anna Vojtech

Then, a rabbit raced by. "This is
a nice place for hiding," she said.
So the rabbit went in and hid.
The mitten puffed up a bit.

Next, a hedgehog came sniffing
by. "This is a nice place for taking
a nap," he said. So the hedgehog
went in and slept. The mitten
puffed up a bit more.

Anna Vojtech

Just then, a big bear came by. "This is a nice place to get warm," he said. So the big bear went in. The mitten puffed up **from** all the animals in it. It puffed up as much as a mitten can.

At last, a black cricket came by. "This is a nice place," he said.

"We do not have **any** space," said the animals in the mitten.

But the black cricket went in. And just as he did…

Anna Vojtech

Rip! Snap! POP!

When Lance came back, there
was not a trace of red mitten left.
So sad!

Cause and Effect

A **cause** is what makes something happen in a story.

An **effect** is the event that happens.

To find the cause and the effect, ask: What happened? Why did it happen?

🔍 Find Text Evidence

Find the causes and effects in the story.

page 57

"Take the mittens and keep them safe," his mom said. But as Lance left, he ran fast and lost a mitten at the edge of the wide forest.

Anna Vojtech

Cause	Effect
Lance ran fast.	He lost his mitten in the forest.
The animals wanted to rest.	The animals went inside the mitten.
Too many animals went in.	The mitten puffed up and got too big.

Your Turn

Talk about the cause and effect of story events in "The Nice Mitten."

Go Digital! *Use the interactive graphic organizer*

Word Choice Page wrote a poem using strong verbs.

Page's Poem

My mom baked a cake.

She mixed, baked, and sliced,

And served it nice and hot.

We will gobble it up on the spot!

Your Turn

- Name the strong verbs in Page's poem.
- What strong verbs will you choose for your poem?

Writers

Past- and Future-Tense Verbs Verbs that end in -**ed** tell about action in the past. Verbs with **will** tell about action in the future.

The verb **baked** is in the past.

The verb **will gobble** is in the future.

My mom **baked** a cake.

We **will gobble** it up.

COLLABORATE

Your Turn

Find other verbs about the past in Page's poem.

Anna Vojtech

67

Essential Question

How is life different than it was long ago?

Go Digital!

Fox Photos/Hulton Archive/Getty Images

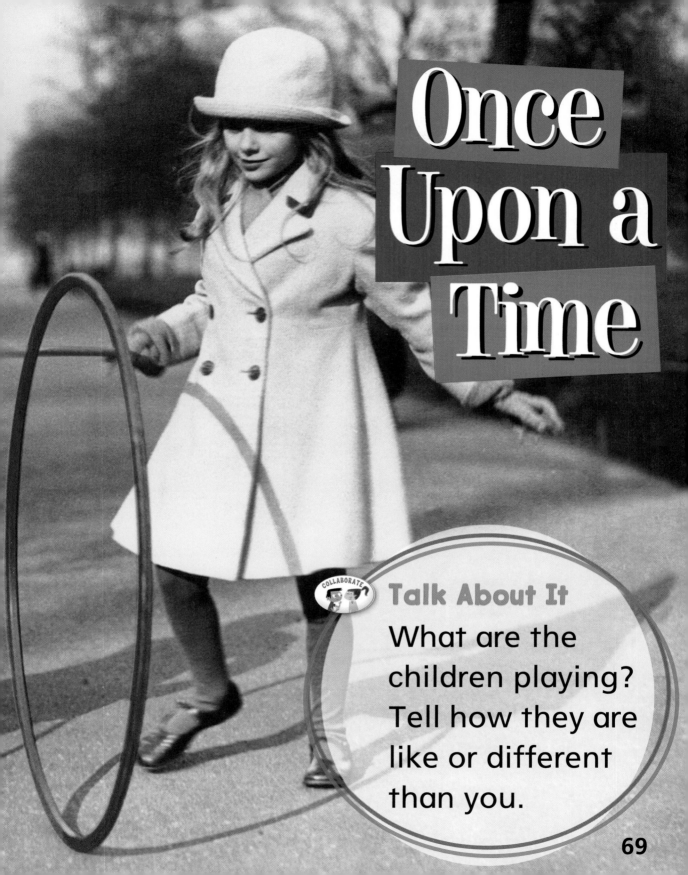

Once Upon a Time

Talk About It

What are the children playing? Tell how they are like or different than you.

ago

Schools were small long **ago**.

boy

That **boy** likes to skate.

girl

This **girl** can ride a bike well.

how

How did kids play in the past?

old

Old homes were made of logs.

people

People went by horse and buggy.

COLLABORATE

Your Turn

Say the sentence for each word. Then make up another sentence.

Go Digital! *Use the online visual glossary*

(tl) VisionsofAmerica/Joe Sohm/Photodisc/Getty Images; (cl) Jupiterimages/Comstock Images/Getty Images; (bl) Don Mason/Blend Images LLC; (tr) Constance Bannister Corp/ Archive Photos/Getty Images; (cr) IS2 from Image Source/ Alamy; (br) Design Pics Inc./Alamy

Long o, u, e

The o_e spelling makes the long o sound in **phone**.

The u_e spelling makes the long u sound in **use**.

The e_e spelling makes the long e sound in **these**.

bone   cute   Eve

drove   hoped   these

Steve   mule   stone

broke   voted   cubes

Valeria Cis

Can Pete use this phone?

Zeke is Rose's cute mule.

Your Turn

Look for these words with o_e, u_e, and e_e in "Life at Home."

home	homes	pole
huge	use	stove
these	those	

Genre Nonfiction

Essential Question

How is life different than it was long ago?

Read about how life at home is different today than it was long ago.

Go Digital!

Life at Home

Has home life changed
a lot since long **ago**?

Yes, it has!

Long ago, many families cooked
worked, and slept in one room.

(bkgd) Siede Preis/Getty Images; The Granger Collection, NYC

Today, families can live in large homes that have lots of space.

A long time ago, homes had just one room. **People** ate and slept in that same room.

Today, homes can have many rooms.

Panorama Productions/Alamy

How did people cook and bake long ago?

A home had a brick fireplace with a pole. A huge pot hung on this pole. People cooked in this big pot.

Long ago, there was an oven at the side of the fireplace. Bread was baked there.

(bkgd) Siede Preis/Getty Images; North Wind Picture Archives

Today, stoves can use gas or electricity.

Now, we use a stove
to cook and bake things.
We still use pots.
But these pots are not
as big as that **old** pot!

(t) William King/The Image Bank/Corbis; (b) Stockbyte/PunchStock

Back then, kids helped out a lot. A **boy** helped his dad plant crops. A **girl** helped her mom inside the home. She made socks and caps. It takes a long time to make those things.

A spinning wheel was used to spin wool into yarn.

(bkgd) Slede Preis/Getty Images; The Granger Collection, NYC

Today, people buy most of the things they need and want.

Now, we shop for things such as socks and caps. We shop for things to eat, as well.

But kids still help out at home.

(t) Image Source/Corbis; (b) Thomas Northcut/Photodisc/Getty Images

Back then, people got water from a well. Then they filled up a big tub and washed things.

In the past, people washed dishes in a tub made of wood.

(bkgd) Siede Preis/Getty Images; The Granger Collection, NYC

Now, people can wash things in a sink. We can wash dishes in a dishwasher, too.

Life is not as hard today as it was long ago!

Today, it's easy to wash dishes in a sink or dishwasher.

Jose Luis Pelaez/Blend Images/age fotostock

Compare and Contrast

When you compare, you think about how things are alike.

When you contrast, you think about how things are different.

 Find Text Evidence

Find out how homes long ago and today are alike and different.

page 77

A long time ago, homes had just one room. **People** ate and slept in that same room.

Today, homes can have many rooms.

Long Ago

Both

Now

Homes had one room.

People live in homes.

Homes have many rooms.

Your Turn

COLLABORATE

Talk about how home life is alike and different in "Life at Home."

Go Digital! Use the interactive graphic organizer

(l) Anne Rippy/Stone/Getty Images; (r) David Buffington/Photodisc/Getty Images

Readers to...

Ideas Pete had an idea about life today. He wrote his opinion.

Pete's Journal Entry

I think computers are great.

Our computer at home is new.

Mom and I are using it to

learn things and play games.

Your Turn

COLLABORATE

- Tell about Pete's opinion and his reasons for it.
- Tell about your idea and your opinion about it.

Writers

Is and Are Use **is** to tell about one thing. Use **are** to tell about more than one thing.

I think computers **are** great.

Our computer at

home **is** new.

Your Turn

COLLABORATE

- Find another sentence with **is** or **are** in Pete's entry.
- Write new sentences with **is** and **are**. Circle **is** and **are**.

Valeria Cis

87

Essential Question
How do we get our food?

Go Digital!

Roland Weihrauch/dpa/Corbis

Food's Journey

COLLABORATE

Talk About It

What happens to farm goods before you eat them?

after

Bread has a crust **after** it is baked.

buy

They **buy** oranges at the store.

done

They are **done** and ready to eat.

every

Every grape is plump and purple.

soon

They will go to the store **soon**.

work

Machines help do the **work**.

Your Turn COLLABORATE

Say the sentence for each word. Then make up another sentence.

Go Digital! *Use the online visual glossary*

(t to b, l to r) Rob Van Petten/Photodisc/Getty Images; Hill Street Studios/age fotostock; Ada Summer/Corbis; Onyx/F1Online; Richard Drury/Photodisc/Getty Images; Bill Stormont/Corbis

oo, u

The letters oo and u can make the sound you hear in the middle of **good** and **push**.

cook	looking	pull
hood	foot	took
hooked	books	wool
put	stood	shook

Holli Conger

Jake put on his wool coat.

He will pull up the hood.

COLLABORATE

Your Turn

Look for these words with oo and u in "A Look at Breakfast."

look	**good**	**put**
full	**cooked**	**pulled**

Essential Question

How do we get our food?

Read about where breakfast foods come from.

Go Digital!

A Look at Breakfast

(bkgd) PhotoLink/Getty Images; The McGraw-Hill Companies, Inc./Ken Cavanagh, photographer

Bread is good for breakfast. But this isn't bread yet. It is wheat. Flour will be made from the wheat.

The wheat is crushed to make flour.

Bloomberg via Getty Images

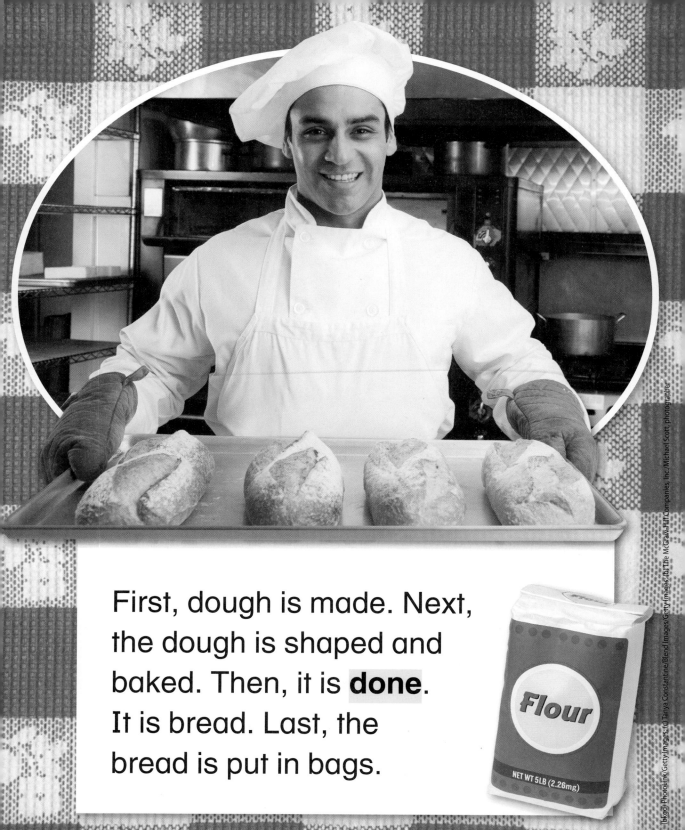

First, dough is made. Next, the dough is shaped and baked. Then, it is **done**. It is bread. Last, the bread is put in bags.

(bkgd) PhotoLink/Getty Images; (c) Tanya Constantine/Blend Images/Getty Images; (b) The McGraw-Hill Companies, Inc./Michael Scott, photographer

Flour

NET WT 5LB (2.26mg)

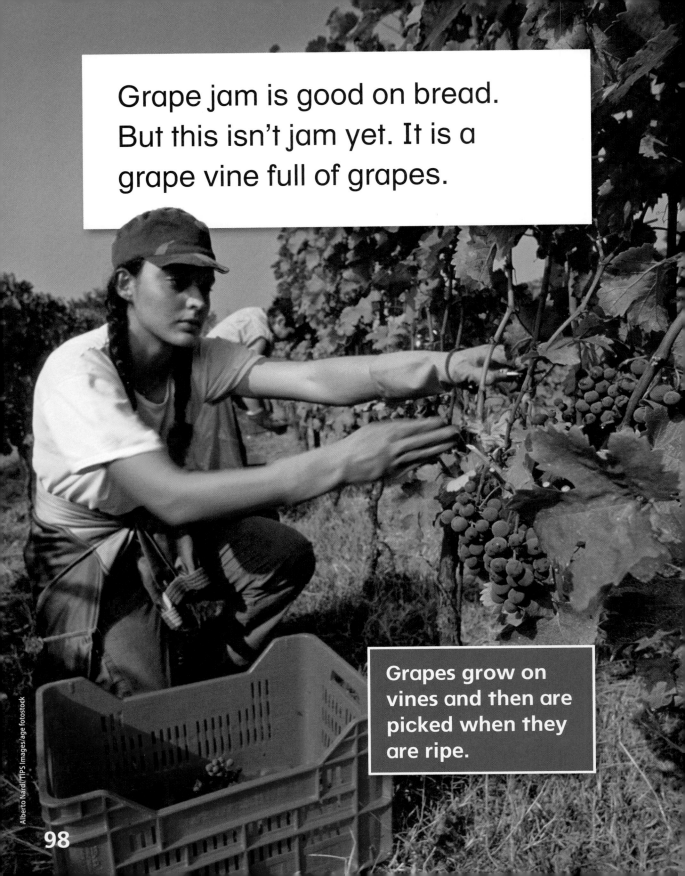

Grape jam is good on bread. But this isn't jam yet. It is a grape vine full of grapes.

Grapes grow on vines and then are picked when they are ripe.

Alberto Nardi/TIPS Images/age fotostock

Trucks take the grapes to a plant. **Every** grape is crushed to make mush. **After** that, the mush is cooked. Now, it is grape jam. Yum!

(bkgd) PhotoLink/Getty Images; (c) Barry Lewis/Alamy; (b) GlowImages/Alamy

Orange juice is good for breakfast, too! Lots and lots of sun makes oranges big and ripe. They will taste good. **Soon**, the big, ripe oranges will get pulled down.

White Star/Monica G/imagebroker/age fotostock

Trucks take piles and piles of oranges to a plant. Then, they get washed. Next, they get crushed. Big sacks get filled with juice.

(bkgd) PhotoLink/Getty Images; (tc) Paulo Fridman/Corbis News/Corbis; (r) Creative Studios/Alamy

The food is shipped in trucks to shops. It is stacked up. Now, it is for sale. People will **buy** it and bring it home. It will make a good breakfast!

(t) Mark Richardson/Alamy; (b) Blend Images/Getty Images

It takes **work** to make food for breakfast.

Food	Where It Comes From	How It Is Made
bread	wheat	Wheat is crushed into flour. Dough is made. Dough is baked into bread.
grape jam	grapes	Grapes are crushed to make mush. Mush is cooked into jam.
orange juice	oranges	Oranges are crushed into juice.

(bkgd) PhotoLink/Getty Images; (t) D. Hurst/Alamy; (c) Photodisc/PunchStock; (b) Stockbyte/Getty Images

Sequence

Authors often give information in **sequence,** or time order. Words such as **first, next, then,** and **last** help you understand the sequence.

🔍 Find Text Evidence

Find the first thing that happens when flour is made into bread.

page 97

First, dough is made. Next, the dough is shaped and baked. Then, it is **done.** It is bread. Last, the bread is put in bags.

Tanya Constantine/Blend Images/Getty Images

104

First

Dough is made.

Next

The dough is shaped and baked.

Then

It is done.

Last

The bread is put in bags.

Your Turn

Talk about how other foods in "A Look at Breakfast" are made. Tell what happens in sequence.

Go Digital! **Use the interactive graphic organizer**

105

D. Hurst/Alamy

 # Readers to...

Ideas Brook had an idea for a topic. She wrote about food.

Brook's Opinion

Food is a fun topic. It isn't dull at all! There are lots and lots of fun facts. I didn't know how grape jam is made. Now I do!

Your Turn COLLABORATE

Tell what reasons Brook gave for her opinion.

Writers

Contractions with not A **contraction** is a short way of writing two words. The contraction **isn't** is a short way of writing **is** and **not**. The apostrophe (') takes the place of the missing letter <u>o</u>.

It **isn't** dull at all!

Your Turn

COLLABORATE

- Find another contraction in Brook's writing. What two words make the contraction?

- Write new sentences. Use contractions with **not**.

Holli Conger